DECLARE HIS GLORY

PREPARATIONS FOR LIFE ON THE MISSION FIELD

SARAH JANE CONAWAY

DEDICATION:

This book is dedicated to anyone who wants to serve the Lord and is willing to learn from Him through this book.

TABLE OF CONTENTS

INTRODUCTION

My purpose for this book comes from people who have asked me various questions about how I became a missionary. My desire is that you will find answers to your questions in this book. Also, I pray that this story of how my husband, Ron and I became missionaries will help someone on their road to serve our Lord Jesus Christ. Those who are not called to go to another country will have a better understanding of what missionaries go through to just get to the their mission field. This story is about the preliminaries that led my husband, Ron, myself and our three sons, Eric, Ron Jr. and Timothy to the foreign mission field.

Just what is a missionary? According to dictionary.com, a missionary is:

1. a person sent by a church into an area to carry on evangelism or other activities, as educational or hospital work.
2. a person strongly in favor of a program, set of principles, etc., who attempts to persuade or convert others.
3. a person who is sent on a mission.

In our work, we were sent out 40 years ago by a local independent Baptist church to tell people in another country, speaking another language, about the Lord Jesus Christ and what He had done for them. We were/are to persuade them to accept Jesus as their Saviour. We should remember that we cannot force people to believe. We simply tell them of His love for them and pray that they will believe in Jesus.

Maybe you don't have an interest in being a missionary but are on the other end of the ministry. Through this book, you will have more insights as to how to pray for missionaries and support them. I will be telling you about our experiences. I have had people tell me that I could not do certain things. They are otherwise known as naysayers. I cite 4 of these in the book. Sometimes naysayers kill dreams and goals of other people, but there are those who go forward anyway. Through the Lord and with the help of my husband I was one of the ones who went forward.

Other missionaries will have a different story to tell. We are all different people and the Lord leads us according to our uniqueness. It is like raising kids. Each one is different and you often use a little different approach from one to the other. I am happy that you are reading this book. Blessings to you as you read. So, let's get into chapter 1.

Sarah Jane Conaway,

Missionary to the Mexican People

My email address is <u>sarahjane@auntjane.ws</u>

I will be happy help to you after you read this book. Just email me. We will take it from there. If you have any questions, just ask.

CHAPTER 1

BEGINNINGS

Hey, honey, didn't you tell me that Harvey and Nellie Underwood had a baby girl the other day?"

"Yes, dear, they named her Sarah Jane."

"Well, the newspaper guys did it again."

"Did what?"

"It says here that the Underwood's had a boy on November 2, 1949 at All Saints Hospital in Fort Worth, Texas."

"Well, she is definitely a cute little girl. At least they got the date and the place of birth right."

This is a probable conversation that could have happened just after I was born between a husband and wife that were friends with my parents. The newspaper had me listed as a boy but that did not make me a boy. Praise the Lord!

I had a sister who was waiting for me to come home to her. Her name is Sylvia Louise. She was 2 years and 9 months old. I could not have asked for a better sister. Our father worked on the railroad as a switchman. His job was to switch the train cars to the track where they needed to go. Our mother was a stay at home mom. Although back then it was rare for mothers to work outside the home. At least it was rare in our neighborhood and among our friends.

Even today, there is nothing wrong with a stay-at-home Mom.

I went to school as any child would and was taught the way the public schools taught children. One thing that made life hard for me was that they taught me to read by sight. I did not learn phonics. I had a very difficult time in school because of that. I did not like to read in public. At times when I did, people would laugh at me because I could not pronounce words correctly. Therefore, I avoided reading aloud. However, I did memorize a lot of words. If I used them often enough I could get by. I did well in math and grammar. These were my favorite subjects. I was an average student and in some classes above average.

My parents raised me in church, especially my mother. Oftentimes, Dad had to work and he also let other things keep him from going to church. For about a year when I was 12-13 years old, I felt an emotion that I did not understand. When we were in church during the invitation I felt like crying and I did. I thought that I must be concerned about other people and their relationship with Jesus, since I as a young child had made a profession of salvation. Then one day when I was in Sunday school my teacher, Sharon McKnight, finished the lesson early. So, she filled in the time with her testimony. She ended her testimony by telling us that if we were not saved, if we did not believe in Jesus and what He did for us on the cross, we would go to Hell. At that point, I knew that I was on my way to Hell. The profession of salvation that I made when I was 6 had not been real. I did not say anything to Sharon. Don't ask me why. I was a teenager. Need I say more? I went to the auditorium for the morning service. Nothing special happened, but in the evening service when Bro. Ramsey preached, he said the same thing that Sharon had said. During the invitation, I went forward. I was crying. In our church, many people went to the altar to pray. I had done it many times myself. Often a friend of mine would join me at the altar and pray for me. This time no one came. I asked the Lord to send someone to me. Thank the Lord, He sent my sister. I told her I was not saved. She called to Bro. Ramsey and he showed me Romans 10:9-10.

⁹ That if thou shalt confess with thy mouth the Lord Jesus, and shalt believe in thine heart that God hath raised him from the dead, thou shalt be saved. ¹⁰ For with the heart man believeth unto righteousness; and with the mouth confession is made unto salvation. (KJV)

At that moment, I accepted what the Lord Jesus Christ did for me on the cross. It became very personal. I mentioned earlier that my sister was the best sister that I could have and this cemented our relationship. After the services my mother told me when I was 6 and had made a profession, she wondered about the reality of it, even though I said everything that I should. She told me that my friend had been saved the week before and had become a member of the church. I did not remember about my friend. However, I did remember wanting to be a member of the church and nothing else was important. I am happy that the Lord spoke to my heart even though it took time for me to realize my spiritual condition.

It was at summer camp, that the Lord called me to give the message of salvation to people who had never heard of Jesus and/or what He had done on the cross for them. People need to have a personal relationship with Jesus. Going to a country where the truth was not known was what the Lord wanted for me. During a Sunday night service after getting back from camp we all gave testimonies of what the Lord had done for us. My parents were happy. They were pleased that I had dedicated my life to serve the Lord. From that moment on, I made plans to become a missionary.

CHAPTER 2

THE DILEMMA

However, there was a dilemma that I had. I had a strong desire to become a nurse. I battled with myself over this apparent problem. At church, I would tell people that I planned to be a missionary. At school I told people including my counselor that I wanted to be a nurse. This went on for a couple of years or so. One day a precious person said to me when I expressed my dilemma, "Why not be both?" It fit! That was the answer to my dilemma. Praise the Lord! From that time on I made plans to go to nursing school.

I graduated from Poly High School in May 1967. I had already applied to Tarrant County Junior College (TCJC). In September of 1967 I entered the nursing program. I was so excited to be doing what I wanted to do. I liked helping people and this was a way to do that. As I entered the house after my first day of college with all my books, my mother said to my dad,

"She'll never make it. There are too many books."

Remember, I was not a good reader. Studying was hard for me, but that statement from my mother stuck with me. My mother taught me a lot about the Lord and about things that a mother teaches her daughter. However, she leaned toward being realistic. Thus, she said, "She will never make it." I was in a class with a lot of brilliant students or at least I thought they were. We all had anatomy and physiology together. It was one combined course. The instructor lectured and everyone took notes the best that they could. I on the other hand took very little legible notes. I was drowning. I guess mother was right.

Some of the students in that class that did not like the way the instructor taught. They claimed that they could listen in class, take notes and transfer that to a test but they did not understand the material. This was way out of my understanding. How could they accomplish all of that and not know the material? When they asked me to join in against the instructor, I simply told them that it was not her fault that I did not understand. I failed the class. It was most devastating. I had never actually failed a class before. I had my problems in school but I always managed to make a passing grade. Of course, failing anatomy and physiology put me out of the nursing program. I did get in one semester of the Fundamentals of Nursing and that got me a job as a nurse's aide. I worked at All Saints Hospital for a while as well as going to TCJC taking basic college courses.

CHAPTER 3
THE WRONG GUY AND THE RIGHT GUY

On a more personal note, my life was not full of dating. I had to adhere to the rules that my parents had set for my sister and me. One of which was that we could not date a boy until we were 16 years old. Then I had to wait for a guy to ask me out. Ugh! We were taught that the boy does the asking, not the girl. So, I waited. I had my first date when I was 17. There were a couple of guys that asked me out occasionally but nothing really serious. I began to realize through the Lord's leading that these guys were not for me. Yes, they were saved and were Baptists, but they were not dedicated to the Lord to do His will for their lives. I broke it off with them. I guess I don't need to go into detail, but I will say that when the last one called me at 9:30 am on Sunday, saying that he had just gotten out of bed and that we could make it for the preaching service, I came unglued! I had told him that my mother was a Sunday school teacher and that she had to ride with us to church. Dad had worked nights and was in bed. My mother did not drive. I had made this clear to him that I was her driver. I canceled all of our dates for my graduation from high school for that next week. My mother was very happy. She was my cheering squad while I was on the phone with him. She did not really like him. So, that was the end of my dating as far as I knew. I would concentrate on guys that had my goal in life of becoming a missionary. I told my mother that I did not want to go through that again. I made a decision not to cry or be discouraged if no one asked me for a date.

A conscious decision for the Lord will never steer you wrong.

About a year later when I was at work at the hospital, on the evening shift, I saw a teen from our church that had recently joined. He was, I thought, at the hospital to visit a patient. A couple of hours later when visiting hours were definitely over, I saw him in the waiting room down the hall from where I was working. I did not understand why he was there and spoke of it to the nurses. They suggested that I go ask him why he was still waiting. I had a hard time with approaching a guy with that kind of a question, but I had to do it. I walked down to the waiting room and he saw me coming and met me half way. I asked him why he was still in the hospital. He said that he came to take me home. I told him that he had not asked me and that my father always came by for me. I told him that I would call home and see if he had left the house yet or not. I called. My sister had answered the phone. My parents had already left. I told my sister that a guy wanted to take me home. She was concerned as to who he was, where did I meet him and was he a Christian. When she understood who he was and that she had worked with him in the deaf ministry at church, she was ok with it. Anyway, my parents met us in the back of the hospital and this guy walked me out to their car. We took him around to the front of the hospital to his car. I left with my parents. It never occurred to me to ask if I could go with him. My parents drove the 20-minute drive to the hospital and it was right that I go with them. However, when we left the parking lot I began complaining and fussing that he would probably never call me. I was so upset. He was the kind of guy that I thought fit my standards. Right in the midst of my ranting, my dear sweet mother asked me a question. **"Are you going to cry?"** Talk about shutting me up. That did! I thought on that for about a minute, remembering what I had said to my mom a year before. With firm determination and a definite reply, I said, "No! If the Lord wants him to call he will call." That was that. No more ranting came from me.

Permit me to tell you a little about this young man. He was from a home where both of his parents were drinkers. They never went to church. One day a pastor came by visiting for Vacation Bible School. He asked this 6-year-old kid if he wanted to go. He didn't know what Vacation Bible School was but it was something to do during the summer. He said, "Yes." He went on Monday and Tuesday. On Wednesday, he accepted Jesus as his Saviour. He went every day that week. This started him in the habit of going to church. He rode the church bus every Sunday. Thus, he was called a bus kid. He was the kind of bus kid that many church leaders had trouble with. He was mischievous. To tell about his escapades would be another book. He did ask his parents frequently to go with him to church, but they refused. Over the years, he had several pastors at Edgewood Baptist in Fort Worth, Texas. Each of them took an interest in him. He learned much from them. He was also a good reader and read his Bible. He realized at a young age that the Lord was calling him to preach the Gospel. He preached his first sermon at the age of 12. Sometime in his youth, the Lord added to that previous call, a call to missions--going to another country to preach the Gospel of our Lord Jesus Christ. The Lord touched his heart with,

"But ye shall receive power, after that the Holy Ghost is come upon you: and ye shall be witnesses unto me both in Jerusalem, and in all Judaea, and in Samaria, and unto the <u>uttermost part of the earth</u>." (Acts 1:8 KJV)

He felt the Lord calling him to <u>the uttermost part of the earth</u>.

Back to the reason for my ranting… he did call me. In fact, he called me often. Ronald A. Conaway and I, Sarah Jane Underwood, were married on June 7, 1969. He was the best thing that ever happened to me apart, of course, from the Lord Jesus Christ.

CHAPTER 4
CHURCH INVOLVEMENT

Before our marriage, when Ron joined our church, he became immediately involved in areas where he was qualified. He knew sign language; therefore, he worked with the deaf. He also took a Sunday School class of ten-year-old boys. One Sunday evening I went forward during the invitation to volunteer to teach Sunday School wherever I was needed. Bro. McClure, the Sunday School Superintendent, said that there was a need for another teacher for the ten-year-old girls. In general assembly there were approximately 20-25 ten-year-old boys and girls. We led the singing in that class. Ron led the boys and I led the girls. We had fun. Bro. McClure had also said that while you both are on a date you might as well visit the kids. So, when we found ourselves near the house of kids that had missed Sunday School on Sunday, we made a visit to see why they had missed. Of course, we also visited kids on regular church visitation. Our church also had a bus ministry. The workers went around on Saturdays inviting kids to go to Sunday School the next day. As I told you earlier Ron had been a bus kid. He had an interest in helping kids who were like him as a child. So, he volunteered to drive a bus. I helped him on his route. It was exciting to see the bus fill up with kids who otherwise would not go to church.

Let me share with you a funny happening one Sunday morning. A member of one of the adult classes asked Ron and I to sing a special for their class. Ron was agreeable to this. However, I was not. We were not talented singers. Yes, we led the kids in singing, but that was different. We practiced with 2 different pianists. Not a good thing to do. The one who played for us during the service added to the music. She did not play that way when we practiced. We sang, "To the Regions Beyond". This is a good song but a hard one for me. We did horribly. No one said anything to us afterwards. I was so embarrassed. As we left the auditorium I was saying that I never ever wanted to sing again. I did not even want to sing in our own Sunday School class. But of course, we did. Just as Ron opened the door, one of the older teachers was trying to lead the singing with the kids. She said, "Oh, I am so glad that you guys are back. Get up here and lead these kids in the songs." We also heard some of the children say, "Now we can really sing!" We went straight to the front of the class and sang with the kids. I realized at that point,that we were where we were meant to be, leading the singing and teaching the 10 year-old children.

God wants you to be yielded to his will. "A man's heart deviseth his way: but the Lord directeth his steps."(Proverbs 16:9 KJV)

Ron's Senior Picture Age 17

Ron and Jane June 7th 1969

The Conaway Family 1979 Taken at

Mount Zion Baptist Church

Jefferson City MO While on Deputation

CHAPTER 5

OUR MARRIED LIFE

After our wedding in June of 1969, we tried to go to Bible College. Ron was 20 and I was 19. Since we both had been living with our own parents, we were unaware of what the freedom of that situation would be. Though we were happy and in love, we were hit hard with the responsibilities of the life on which we had then embarked. We had no one to tell us what to do or when to get up in the mornings. I had actually thought that I was rather disciplined but when the circumstances changed, so did the reality of actual discipline. We did not make it in Bible College. Basically, because we did not get up and go to school. Working late then getting up early was a trial. This carried over to Sundays as well.

We needed to learn to parent ourselves and be responsible.

I still wanted to become a nurse. After dropping out of Bible College, I applied to a 3-year nursing program. It was with the hospital where I was working. I was not accepted. I felt so let down. The nursing supervisor of the floor where I worked came to me and said,

"This nursing school is not the only one. Don't drop this dream of becoming a nurse just because one school said no. Keep applying till one accepts you."

Well, that did help me a little. However, if you remember, I had failed anatomy and physiology and now I was rejected. Ok, I put the failure and rejection on the back burner as well as pursuing a nursing degree.

Soon after that we moved to Waco, TX and got jobs in a local hospital. Through this hospital we found out about a nursing program at the community college. So, Ron and I both applied to this one. We were both accepted! Wow! The third time trying to fulfill my dream was here. Now to study and to pass all my courses was my goal. Ron was a much better student than I was. He was a good reader from the beginning of his schooling. He encouraged me often and helped me when he could. He would study and remember almost everything. He took steps to help his assigned patients. He had studied about their condition and was able to give them a degree of comfort. He even charted that he had alleviated one patient's fear of surgery. This was not acceptable with our instructors. They told him that he was stepping beyond his position as a nursing student; he could not have alleviated the patient's fear. He told them to go ask the patient. We never heard if they did or not. In class, he began asking questions that the instructors could not answer. Eventually, they asked him to drop out of nursing. They said that he acted like a frustrated medical student and told him to go to medical school. This was shocking to me because his grades were much better than mine. However, he did as they suggested. He dropped out of nursing. We realized years later that he should have insisted on staying in the program, but that became hindsight. He did stay in the junior college and continued to take science courses.

At the end of the second semester of our first year my mother called us. She asked me if I passed all my classes. I told her that we both did. Her response to that was, "I'm not worried about Ron. It is you that I am worried about." Thanks, Mom! Would I ever be smart in my mother's opinion? It really hurt me. I learned a lot from my mother growing up. I remember much of that, but she had a viewpoint that we should accept things the way they are, which, in my case, was to accept my lack of ability to learn. When I told Ron what she had said, he told me that I would make an A in chemistry in our summer classes. I told him that I couldn't do that especially since he had just made a B in it that spring semester. Well, that summer I made that A in chemistry! What an encouragement that was to me! I continued in the nursing program and I passed everything. Praise the Lord! Without the Lord, I would not have been able to accomplish it.

While still in junior college, we had gotten almost completely out of church. This burdened me. I remember talking to the Lord when I was home alone. Now this was not a down on your knees kind of talk. I was working in the house and thinking of our situation. I was remembering the reason that I had married Ron. It was because he wanted to be a missionary. He had said a few days earlier that he did not think that he would ever preach again. I was broken hearted but I did not know how to change the situation.

I had to do something, but nothing came to mind.

I did not realize it at the time that I was doing something. As I worked in the house doing things that did not take concentration, **I was actually praying.** My devotional life was nonexistent. Well, the Lord did answer those prayers of mine. He worked on Ron's heart. The Lord got his attention one night while Ron pulled a double at the hospital and wound up in an undesirable place.

The Lord asked him, "Man of God what are you doing in a place like this?"

Ron spent that night reviewing his life and what the Lord had said. He reaffirmed his salvation and his call to the ministry. The next day when he came home, he told me all that had happened. He also said that we were getting back into church to do what the Lord had called us to do. It was so refreshing to be back in church following God's call, doing what we both had dreamed about years before.

From this point on, we were on our road to serving the Lord on the mission field. Let me insert here one thing for you, the reader.

If you are planning your life to serve the Lord always remember that the choices you make no matter how small can derail you from your calling.

We had made several that derailed us, but praise the Lord He put us back on track.

CHAPTER 6

PASTORING IN MARLIN, TEXAS

R on's father told him about a church that needed a pastor. Sometime during Ron's childhood his parents had received the Lord and his father became a student of the Bible. He also became a lay preacher. He was given the chance to preach occasionally by his pastor. He had filled the pulpit in Marlin, Texas at Eastside Baptist Church. Ron was ecstatic about the possibility of pastoring. It had been almost a year since we were back in church and he was ready to do more. I, on the other hand, sat there thinking that I was not ready to be a pastor's wife. I wanted to go to Bible College first. Well, he contacted the people at the church and they scheduled a Sunday morning service for him to preach in view of call. I was ok with this. Just because he was given the chance to preach did not mean that he would be called to pastor. Well, as it turned out, he received the call from the members to be their pastor. I was in a state of shock. However, I did believe that the wife should support her husband in the ministry as well as in life. So, that was that. The pastor from the church in Temple that we were members of gave Ron some advice. He said, "This church has been through a lot of pastors, you will not hurt it. Just don't stay so long that it hurts you." I don't know that we took that statement fully to heart. We felt that anyone could do harm, including us. So, we prayed that that would not happen. However, the last part of the statement really meant something to us. Many of the previous pastors had left after a big problem in the church. We found out later that the members were of the opinion that pastors only left when there was a problem.

After Ron took the pastorate, we were driving from Temple to Marlin for services until we could move. We usually stayed in Marlin for the entire day. One Sunday in particular we were having Sunday dinner with a family of the church. I was helping the lady in the kitchen with the meal. While we were getting things ready, we were talking. She told me that I needed to tell my husband not to preach about a certain subject because she had a friend that came to church occasionally and that it would offend her. I simply told her that I had no authority to tell my husband what to preach. That was between him and the Lord. The Lord had called my husband Ron to preach. It was not my place to tell him what to say or not to say. Yes, of course, there were times I offered suggestions, but he made the decision to use it or not. I accepted his decision as being from the Lord.

We became accustomed to the responsibilities of a pastor. Agreed, it was a small church and it did not have the complexities of larger ones. It was Ron's first pastorate. It was experience that we needed to continue our road to the mission field. Most of the members were senior adults. Only a couple of families had young children. I had a hard time understanding how these seniors could listen to this young man preach, when they knew so much more than he did. After all, they had been Christians longer than we had been alive. How could Ron teach them anything that they did not already know? Well, my friend, it did not take me long to realize that the number of years that you are a Christian does not indicate that you have accumulated knowledge of the Word of God. There needs to be personal devotionals in the individual's life for spiritual growth to happen. I really began to realize that Ron had a lot of real Bible training from his pastors when he was young. He also read the Bible for himself. He studied and he had been preaching since he was 12 years old. I really began to enjoy listening to my husband preach and I learned so much from him.

Well, life was happening to us in Marlin. I finished nursing school the summer after Ron took the pastorate. I was scheduled to take state boards in October that year. They told us what color the envelope would be if we passed and what color it would be if we did not pass. I kept that information to myself. I wanted to be the first to know.

Life continued to happen; I was 8 months pregnant when I sat for boards. Most people could not tell that I was expecting and it was not something that I waved a flag about. Much different from the way things are done now in the 21st century. I prayed about the delivery of my child. The baby could not be born on Sunday or Wednesday or at any other time that would take Ron away from the church. We had no one to preach in his place. There were many other things that I prayed about as well as the birth of our new little arrival. He made his entrance into our lives on Tuesday, November 20, 1973 at 4 a.m. We were so happy we had a son. He was a healthy 8 lb. baby. The Lord answered all my prayers for this baby in the positive. We had gone to the hospital at 2 a.m. No church services at that hour of the night!

Two days after Eric's arrival, Ron went out to get the mail. He had an envelope in his hand from the State Board of Nursing in Austin, Texas. He had promised me that he would not open it. He brought it to me. I saw the brown envelope! I could not believe it! I opened it. I read the letter and my license! I had passed! Then I noticed something very special. They had signed my license on Eric's birthday. So, since today Eric is 43 (at the time of this writing) I have been a nurse for 43 years! Praise the Lord! So, contrary to what some people thought, I did become a registered nurse.

A few months later Ron was feeling like he was ready to leave Marlin and the church. We had several people saved during that year but all of them were in Marlin visiting family. Some were children and others were adults. We had visited every house in that small town. Ron felt that the Lord was telling him it was time to leave. At that time, there were no problems in the church. The people could not understand why we wanted to leave. What was wrong? Nothing was wrong. It was just time to go. So, we began to pray specifically – go where and do what?

We had bought a mobile home when we moved to Marlin. Soon after we had begun praying about where to go and what to do, we received a phone call from a new mobile home park in Belton, Texas. They offered to move us and give us the first month free for the lot. Ron and I were excited. It was the thing to do. This mobile home park was behind Mary-Hardin Baylor University. Ron was interested in applying there to finish his nursing. However, this was a Baccalaureate program in nursing. I had graduated with an Associate degree. Ron applied and was accepted. They encouraged his questions. He was able to transfer his courses from the junior college and other courses he challenged.

We also returned to the membership of the church in Temple, Texas where we had been before his pastorate.

CHAPTER 7

LIFE PREPARATIONS CONTINUE

Ron was in school full force even though it was a week into the semester. He was right where he needed to be. He was learning so much more than he would have in the Associate degree program. He had classes mostly in the daytime but he also had some of them on Tuesday and Thursday nights. He also worked as an orderly at the Santa Fe Railroad Hospital part-time in the evenings. I worked there at night full time. We were happy that we had responded to the Lord's leading. Everything seemed to be falling into place for our future as missionaries.

Our church work became more involved. Our pastor asked Ron to start a junior church with only 3 church kids. Our church had visitation on Tuesday nights and Thursday nights. We could choose which one we could attend. It was a time that we went out telling people about the Lord, encouraging Christians who were having problems and visiting the sick and praying with them. As I said above, Ron was in class on Tuesdays and Thursdays so he could not visit on those evenings. I was able to attend both. Ron and I visited on Fridays and Saturdays. We either hired a babysitter to watch Eric or we packed him with us. We did this so that Ron could visit for the junior church. I was visiting 3-4 times a week and

Ron twice a week. This is why our junior church grew to 50 children in 2 years.

We had a puppet ministry with the kids. Ron had a puppet who was the pastor and among others I had Preacher Pup. The first time I spoke for the puppet I had tried to memorize the script. I messed up and during the program I stuttered really badly, because I could not remember my lines. The next Sunday I was better prepared, so I did not stutter. The kids were asking why Preacher Pup did not stutter. So, I had to stutter from then on to please the kids. We had so much fun with them and saw many kids come to Christ. One church kid had memorized the books of the Bible. He was really good with his memory verses, too. He wanted to know what else he could study. Ron told him to memorize the books of the Bible backwards. He did it! Praise the Lord!

A missionary from Papua New Guinea came to our church to present his ministry. This presentation caught Ron's eyes and his heart. He began to study about the country. One day in the library at Mary-Hardin Baylor University in Belton, Texas Ron was studying for a lecture that he was to present to some high school students. He became tired of studying and laid down his work for a few minutes and picked up a *National Geographic* magazine which boasted an article on Papua New Guinea. As Ron read that article the author was calling Papua New Guinea the "uttermost part of the earth."

The Lord said to him, "Son that is where I want you to go.

That country is your uttermost."

From that time on we made plans to go to Papua New Guinea as missionaries.

One night after church, the pastor told Ron that he was burdened about some things and wanted prayer. Ron agreed. He told me about it and we decided to call a prayer meeting in our home. After we got home, we called the pastor at the church first and there was no answer, so we called his home. Again, there was no answer. We continued to call other people to pray for the pastor and his unspoken request to cover him with the strength of the Lord. Many people came. We continued to try to reach the pastor but were unsuccessful. We had the prayer meeting and everyone left. A day or two later the pastor and his wife came by to talk to us about that meeting. They were accusing us of doing something wrong and were asking why they were not included in the meeting. I told them repeatedly that we called and no one answered the phone. They insisted that we did not call. I know that we did several times. (By the way, this was in 1975 long before caller ID and the ability to leave messages.) I became angry, very angry. Why would they not believe us?

Then the pastor's wife said,

"Jane, you will keep your husband off the mission field because of your temper."

Here it goes again, someone telling me I can't or won't be able to do something. My husband told me, "They do not know that you have been seeking the Lord's help with controlling your temper. They don't know that you have memorized Psalms 19:14."

"Let the words of my mouth, and the meditation of my heart, be acceptable in thy sight, O LORD, my strength, and my redeemer." (KJV)

I pray that if you, the reader, have a problem with anger, you will go to the Lord with it. There are many verses in the Bible that will help you overcome it or any other sin that is a trial for you. We are all sinners as the Bible says in Romans 3:23. We cannot stop serving the Lord because we have a problem with sin. Hello, we all do. By the way, I have friends that can't believe that I ever had a problem with my temper. I also have a friend from high school, Sandy, who told me just a few years ago that she could not believe how I had changed. She was surprised that I was not angry when my car died and was irreparable.

Prayer and Scripture do work. However, it takes willingness to see the problem and to do something about it.

CHAPTER 8
PREPARATIONS IN BIBLE COLLEGE

Ron felt that he did not need to go to Bible College. He had been studying his Bible so much more than I had as a young person. I was the one who wanted to study more. I prayed for him to change his mind. In the spring semester of his last year of his nursing, he changed his mind. We applied to Bible College again. This time we had a really strong desire to prepare ourselves for our future ministry. Eric was 2 years old at the beginning of our Bible College days. I guess I am saying that we were more responsible as adults at 26 than we were at 19, but we all do grow up. At least I hope so. Ron wanted to take state boards in the state where the Bible College was. That way he could get a nursing job quicker. We prepared to move and actually did move. We did not expect anything but acceptance into the school. Therefore, we did not wait for the acceptance letter. This was in hindsight a good thing. I will explain later.

The Bible College had a practice that the pastors of incoming students were to send a private letter of recommendation to the president of the school. At least normally it was private. The letter our pastor sent was not a recommendation. We heard from the office staff that there was a problem between us and our sending pastor. Ron said that he did not know anything about it. We called our pastor. When Ron told him of the rumor, he denied the existence of a problem. In plain and simple words, he lied to Ron. The president finally called Ron into his office and told him that there was a letter full of accusations against the both of us. He continued to say that he felt that Ron had the right to defend himself. The letter was read in part to Ron. It mentioned that Ron never went on visitation. Ron explained that he had classes on the two nights of church wide visitation. He also explained what I have already mentioned in the previous chapter about how we both visited apart from church organized visitation. Of course, it was written about my temper. Remember I told you that the pastor's wife said that I would keep Ron off the mission field. Well, they were doing their best to make that become a reality. Ron shared with the president how that I was working on that problem by praying and memorizing Scripture. There was a whole lot more that I don't care to go into. Ron was sure that the president did not tell him everything either. So, the conclusion to this situation was an act by the president. He pitched the letter into file 13. He also stated that he would watch us during our first year at the school. This sounded reasonable to my husband. We were accepted into college!

If we had not been there in person,

the president might have just sent us a letter rejecting our application.

During that second semester of our Bible college days, the President was overwhelmed with a debilitating disease,

Myasthenia Gravis. He was in intensive care for a period of time, then he was moved to the step-down unit. Guess who his nurse was? Yes, that is right. It was my husband, Ron. As long as the president was on Ron's floor they had long talks after Ron got off work at 11 pm. The two men got very well acquainted. So much so, that in Ron's last semester of school he wanted Ron to start and head an infirmary at the college. Ron shared the offer with me and we agreed that the Lord did not call us to begin an infirmary. He called us to be missionaries in Papua New Guinea.

During our first semester in Bible College, our second son was born. We named him after my husband. He is Ronald Arnett Conaway Jr. We never thought that we would name a son junior but that was the only name that fit. While he was growing up, he was more like his dad than Eric. However, now they both look like daddy, just not as big.

During the time we were in school, I had an instructor for one of my teaching classes, who gave the class a test that I will never forget. It was all matching which under normal circumstances was ok. However, the blanks on the left could have multiple answers from the right side. Also, the right column had less answers in them. Each one could be used more than once. There was no way to know how many should be in each blank or how many times each answer was to be used. I did not like the test. The most answers that I put on one blank was 4. I felt like I could have missed some of them. I told the teacher that I did not like the test.

She told me that I would not make it on the mission field because I did not like change.

Here we go again, someone telling me that I would not make it on the field, but as before it did not stop me from training or planning for the field.

I had another instructor in Bible College that encouraged us to find a Scripture verse that would direct us to where we wanted to go. That led me to find Psalm 96:3

"Declare his glory among the <u>heathen</u>, his wonders among all people." (KJV)

The word heathen spoke to me. I wanted to give the message of salvation to the heathen of Papua New Guinea. I was happy that the Lord gave me that verse. Hey, the story does not stop there. When you ask the Lord for something He gives you more than you ask for. One day while we were on deputation we were in a mission conference in south Texas. We were listening to a Filipino pastor preach. As I was following him in his sermon he came to Psalm 2:8,

"Ask of me, and I shall give thee the <u>heathen</u> for thine inheritance, and the <u>uttermost parts of the earth</u> for thy possession."

I stared at that verse for a few minutes. It had been about 2 years since I had asked the Lord for a verse on which to base my call. Now He gave me another verse for the mission field.

The Lord will give us <u>the heathen</u> upon our asking and the <u>uttermost parts of the earth</u> for our possession. Do you remember that Ron wanted to go to the <u>uttermost part of the earth</u>?

How good is that! The Lord put my verse and Ron's verse together into one verse. Praise His Name!

CHAPTER 9

DEPUTATION

What is deputation? This is a period of time set aside for the missionary to build financial support to pay for all the needs necessary to build the church on his mission field until that church is self-supporting. It is also for maintaining himself and his family on the foreign field. The length of deputation varies with each missionary family. Some take as little as 2 years and others 4 years or more.

The process of getting appointments is a big part of the life of the missionary. In January 1978 phone calls were very expensive. One call could be $2-$5 depending on the length of the call. This was before the long-distance phone companies and especially before the unlimited calling of our cell phones. Ron would begin to make calls to pastors from a list he had acquired of Independent Baptist Churches. Many were unable to invite a missionary to speak to their church because of lack of funds. It cost a ton of money in phone calls before we got our first appointment. I would sit with Ron, ready with a calendar and a pen. I would take notes as he talked if he got an appointment. We needed to verify the address, the time of services, and when the pastor wanted us to arrive. Ron would tell him if we needed accommodations. We also had to have a map to plan the distance between churches especially on Sundays. We started getting appointments close to where we were living so that we could return home after the services unless of course the pastor wanted us to stay over. When we bought a motor home we only needed hook-ups for it. We moved into the motor home towards the end of our first-year of traveling. This was very helpful in cutting expenses. Yes, a motor home uses a lot of gas, but we did not have a car or a house anywhere. So, our utilities became the gas in the motor home. Most of the time we were allowed to plug into the electricity at the church and stay there past the appointment date for a night or two until it was time for us to go to our next appointment.

Once we arrived at a church for the service, I would set up a display of our mission field. Ron would be talking with the pastor about what he wanted him to do–give a testimony, show slides of the mission work and/or preach. The pastor would tell him how much time he should take. If there was enough time allowed I gave a short testimony. The slide presentation took a lot of time to prepare long before we ever went to a church. We had slides and a projector. Ron would talk as he went through the slides. He had to be careful not to take too long. Now days it is so much easier to have a presentation of 10 minutes or less pre-recorded on a CD or memory chip.

Once we presented our ministry at a church, they would vote during a designated time on the missionaries that had been there. Often, we did not know if they would support us until the pastor wrote to us, called us or just simply started supporting. Every church is different as to how they vote on supporting missionaries. There were times that the pastor would tell Ron ahead of time that they were not able to take on any more missionaries but the church could give a love offering to help us on to the next church. If we did not have an appointment on a Sunday or Wednesday we would drop in for services at a church just as visitors. Many times, Ron was allowed to give a testimony. I remember one church that we dropped in on, on a Sunday morning. We had the motor home and Ron was sick with fever. He thought about staying in the home while the boys and I went in but he changed his mind, because that seemed odd to him to be in the parking lot of the church and not go inside. We walked in just after the first song and the pastor asked him who we were. Ron told him and then the pastor said why don't you just come on up here and preach for us. Ron went up to do what he enjoyed doing – preaching. I sat in my place praying for him because I knew how bad he felt.

There were some pastors that could not take us on for support but said that they would pay our air passage to the field. So, Ron would call that pastor a few months ahead of our departure date. Others would supply some equipment that was needed.

During our first year of our deputation, I was expecting our third son, Timothy. He was born in October of 1978. When he was in my room for the first time after delivery, I noticed that his lips were blue. The nurse said that it was normal and not to be concerned about it. However, there were tests done and the preliminary diagnosis was pneumonia. He was admitted to the newborn intensive care unit. The nurses did not tell me until it was time for the babies to be given to the mothers for feeding. My roommate got her baby but the nurse told me that mine was in newborn intensive care. Nothing more was said to me. I laid there crying. My husband in the meantime came to visit and before he saw me he was taken to the intensive unit. He was with our baby for about an hour when a nurse in the newborn intensive unit asked him why I was not in there. He said that he did not know. So, another nurse from the unit came and got me. I could have been with my baby the whole time but no one told me. The 24 and 48-hour lab cultures came back negative and the doctor on consult stated that he felt that a lung had just not inflated sufficiently and that it just appeared to be pneumonia. However, the 72-hour lab cultures came back grade B strep. This we were told was 98% fatal with newborns. Timothy was already getting better when we found this out. The doctor on consult did not understand it. Our doctor was a Christian and he totally understood it. Prayers had been going up for our baby. We took him home a week after his birth with an antibiotic and liquid calcium. After finishing the calcium we called the doctor to see if we needed to continue it or not. He gave a script but the pharmacist was unfamiliar with this dose for an infant, but he filled. The supplement was thick. The instructions were the same. I gave it to my baby not knowing that it was too much calcium. My 2-week old son, Timothy, was sleeping 6-8 hours at a time. I had to wake him up to feed him. On October 28th, a Saturday, I was home alone with my 2 younger sons. I was holding Timothy and we had a prayer meeting together. I prayed for my son. Why was he sleeping so much? The next day after the prayer meeting my baby was more alert in between medication times. There had not been any change with his medications. That Sunday afternoon, Ron and Eric returned home from a church where he presented our mission call. I told Ron about what had happened and that when I gave the last dose of the antibiotic I was not giving the baby any more calcium. He promised me that he would not tell the doctor. Monday morning Timothy was alert and better than ever since we had him home with us. Well, on Thursday we took him to the lab for blood work which included his calcium level which was extremely high. The lab doctor told us that if I had given Timothy just one more dose of calcium he would have gone into a coma. Wow! The Lord gave Timothy to us on the 11th of October. On Saturday the 14th it was discovered that he had grade B strep pneumonia, he recovered only to be overdosed with calcium and almost going into a coma. Praise the Lord for his guidance and for answering prayer on Saturday October 28, 1978. All of this happened in about 3 weeks in the midst of our deputation.

Serving the Lord is not without trials. Through these trials, we are made strong. We learn to depend on our Lord and Saviour Jesus Christ.

We were in about 400 or more churches while on deputation. Sunday morning, Sunday night and Wednesday night were the usual times for presenting our ministry. We were also in mission conferences that usually lasted Wednesday through Sunday. In one conference in which we participated, there was another missionary to Papua New Guinea present. We were excited to see him and hear about the country to which we had been called. We invited him into our motor home one afternoon between the services. He spent 2 hours with us telling us about Papua New Guinea. One thing he said really hit me hard.

He said that I would not make it in the bush of Papua New Guinea because I was born and raised in the city.

Of all the times that people had said that I could not do something, this one affected me the most. When he left that afternoon, I was convinced that I could not be a missionary in the bush of Papua New Guinea. It took Ron about 2 weeks to make me realize that **if God called me, I could do it.** Praise the Lord for my husband and the promises of our Lord.

We continued building our support to go to the field of Papua New Guinea. The deputation road is hard. Some missionary families are separated during that time. The husband goes on the road alone. Whether the whole family goes on the road or just the husband, it is hard. Yet, it is full of blessings as well. I have many friends across America because I traveled with my husband. We were able to encourage each other along the way. Traveling in a 25-foot motor home for 2 years or more is not a vacation with 3 small children in it, but we were all together experiencing new things as a family.

Chapter 10

You Can't

There was a minimum of 4 times that people said that I could not do something that I felt the desire or the calling to do. This is a review of those statements that I have already mentioned.

1. You will never become a nurse.   I did become a nurse. (Chapter 2)

2. Your temper will keep you off the mission field. For 40 years I have been a missionary as of January 2018. (Chapter 7)

3. You will not make it on the mission field because you don't like change. Again, I say that I have been a missionary for 40 years. This is not to say that I liked changes that happened to us, but the Lord gave me grace to get through them. (Chapter 8)

4. You are a city girl. You can't make it in the bush of Papua New Guinea. (Chapter 9) Where does this leave the Lord?

He calls and He enables.

I once told a missionary friend, Sharon, in Mt. Hagen, Western Highlands Province, Papua New Guinea, that I was one step closer to the bush than she was. She informed me that I was more than one step closer to the bush. She added, you have been here so long that you just don't realize how close you are to the bush. Another illustration to this one is a conversation I had with a pastor's wife in Milwaukee, Wisconsin. I told her what the missionary said about not being able to make it in the bush of Papua New Guinea. She informed me that she was raised in the country and at that time she was in the city of Milwaukee doing what the Lord wanted her to do. She had only one small patch of grass that she cultivated and made something of it.

I guess you can say that the Lord often takes us out of our comfort zones to make us what He wants us to be.

I have listed these here to prove a point. Just because someone says something about you does not make it true. I heard a lecture the other day which said, "Don't let what someone says about you become a reality." I would like to say,

Become the reality the Lord wants for you.

CHAPTER 11
MESSAGE TO THE READERS

What will it be for you? Will you follow the Lord no matter the cost? Keep up your daily devotions, keep learning to follow Him in all that you do and you will make it to the mission field.

1. If you are young, remember that all that you do in your work life is a contribution to your knowledge that can be used on the field.

2. If you are a senior citizen, consider going to a mission field to help a seasoned missionary for a short term – a few weeks or months. Your talents and experience could be just what they need to enhance their ministry. The Lord can use you at whatever age you are with whatever talents you have.

3. For those of you who are not called to go. Make a plan to pray for the missionaries that your church supports and other missionaries as well.

Now that you have read this book maybe you will be able to understand that there are trials that the missionaries are going through that are not publicized. Pray for them regularly. They need it. Pray for us. Two of my 3 sons and I are on the field.

We need your prayers. I pray that this book has answered some of your questions and has given you insight into a few of one missionary family's experiences in preparation for the mission field.

Blessings to you and to your families,

Sarah Jane Conaway, "Aunt Jane"

Serving Jesus in Mexico

sarahjane@auntjane.ws

Since you have finished the book, let me help you. Just email me at the above address.

About the Author

Sarah Jane Conaway has been a Christian for over 55 years. In that time she has taught Sunday School and ladies classes. He has also taught classes on how to teach Sunday School. She has counseled ladies on how they should be a wife and mother. She has spoken to ladies groups and in churches about their ministries. She and her husband, Ron Conaway Sr. and their three sons, Eric, Ron Jr. and Timothy were missionaries to Papua New Guinea in the South Pacific for 16 years. Their ministry moved to Mexico in 1995 where they are currently ministering. Ron graduated to Heaven in January 2005. She and her oldest son, Eric, have continued with the ministry.

ACKNOWLEDGMENTS

I want to sincerely thank Eric, my oldest son, who worked with me in the editing and gave me so much encouragement along the way. I want to say thank you to Timothy, my third son, for all of those meals that you prepared so that I could get this book completed. Thank you, Ronald Jr., my second son, for the encouragement you gave me when I told you about the writing of this book. I also want to express my appreciation to Karen Milligan. You went beyond editing with all of your words of encouragement. I feel so privileged to have you with me in this new project. I want to say that I feel that my late husband, Ron, is in heaven cheering me on as he did when I was working at something new when he was here with us. Rielle Moises, you have been such a wonderful accountability buddy. You have helped me so much. Thank you.

Do you want to write a book?

Don't know how?

Want to learn how to self-publish?

Let me recommend you to my school,

You will receive a $250 discount for going through me.

Send me 4 things via this email address

sarahjane@auntjane.ws

Your first and last names

Your phone number

Your email address

How do you know me?

For example: via this book or if in person give a few details.

www.ingramcontent.com/pod-product-compliance
Lightning Source LLC
Chambersburg PA
CBHW060431050426
42449CB00009B/2241